A History of Britain

CROWNS, PARLIAMENTS AND PEOPLE

1500–1750

Richard Dargie

W

FRANKLIN WATTS

LONDON • SYDNEY

First published in 2008 by Franklin Watts

Franklin Watts
338 Euston Road
London NW1 3BH

Franklin Watts Australia
Level 17/207 Kent Street, Sydney, NSW 2000

Produced by Arcturus Publishing Limited,
26/27 Bickels Yard, 151–153 Bermondsey Street, London SE1 3HA

Series concept: Alex Woolf
Editor and picture researcher: Patience Coster
Designer: Phipps Design

Picture credits:
akg-images: 10, 12, 17 and cover, 19, 20, 22.
Corbis: 8 (The Gallery Collection), 28 (top, Bettmann).
Getty Images: 23.
Mary Evans Picture Library: 26, 27, 28 (bottom).
The Bridgeman Art Library: 4 (The Stapleton Collection), 6 (Ken Welsh), 7 (Ken Welsh), 11 (The Stapleton Collection), 16, 18 and cover (Museum of London, UK), 25 and cover (Guildhall Library, City of London).

A CIP catalogue record for this book is available from the British Library.

Dewey Decimal Classification Number: 941.05

ISBN 978 0 7496 8196 8

Printed in China

Franklin Watts is a division of Hachette Children's Books.

Contents

 # 1485–1547

Kings of the Early Modern Age

The victory of the Welsh prince, Henry, at the Battle of Bosworth in 1485 heralded the start of the Tudor age. Over the course of time, the two countries of England and Scotland joined to become a single united kingdom. This new British state was powerful in wealth and influence and staunchly Protestant in faith.

In 1486 Henry Tudor married Elizabeth of York. This united the Houses of Lancaster and York after many years of war.

Henry Tudor

Henry Tudor ruled as Henry VII from 1485–1509. He inherited an England that had been exhausted and bankrupted by three decades of civil war. Henry's first task was to put the royal finances in order. By the end of his reign, the Crown's income had almost tripled to over £140,000 each year. Henry knew that England's prosperity also relied on peace with his neighbours, so he arranged for his daughters to marry into the royal families of Scotland and France.

Star Chamber

Henry was determined to limit the power of the English nobles. He introduced new laws against keeping large households of armed men, so putting an end to the private armies of the great lords. Henry also used the Court of Star Chamber to speed up legal cases that had ground to a halt in local courts, where powerful nobles often put pressure on judges and witnesses. Meeting in secret, men loyal to the king ran the Star Chamber and decided cases without calling witnesses or juries. There was no appeal against its decisions, even for the most noble of defendants.

Timeline

1485	• Henry Tudor defeats Richard III at Bosworth
1488	• James IV becomes King of Scotland
1509	• Henry VIII succeeds to the English throne
1513	• James IV dies in battle at Flodden Field
1530s	• Henry breaks with Rome and creates the Church of England
1536	• Northern rising against Henry VIII's religious policies
1540s	• England bankrupted by Henry's wars

4

James IV

James IV ruled Scotland from 1488–1513. A gifted linguist, he founded St Leonard's College in St Andrews, established Scotland's third university at King's College in Aberdeen and set up the first Scottish printing press in Edinburgh. James passed a law in 1496 that required all wealthy men to educate their sons at grammar school until they had learned 'perfect Latin'. The king's interest in science resulted in the foundation of the Royal College of Surgeons in 1505, and in the establishment of modern gun foundries and dockyards. His flagship *The Great Michael*, launched in 1511, was the largest European ship of its day, weighing over 1,000 tons and carrying 300 guns.

Henry VIII

Henry VIII succeeded his father Henry VII as King of England and ruled from 1509–47. His reign began well – the young king was described as athletic and intelligent. In time, however, Henry's lack of interest in government meant that he relied too much upon favourite ministers. His lack of a son led to difficulties in his marriages. Religious troubles boiled over in the Pilgrimage of Grace in 1536. This was a rebellion of northern Catholics who were unhappy at Henry's break with the Church of Rome. There then followed unsuccessful and unprofitable wars in Scotland and France in the 1540s, which bankrupted the English Crown.

Henry VIII is remembered mainly as a brutal husband and ruthless king, but he was also a learned man and a great patron of the arts.

Henry's Wives

Henry's first marriage to the Spanish princess, Catherine of Aragon, produced a daughter, as did Henry's second marriage to Anne Boleyn. His favourite wife was Jane Seymour, who gave birth to a son. However, the executions of Boleyn and Catherine Howard (Henry's fifth wife) were signs that Henry had turned into a cruel tyrant.

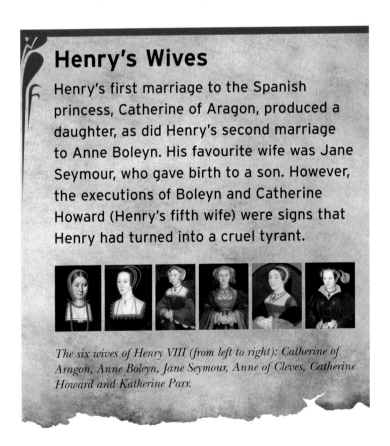

The six wives of Henry VIII (from left to right): Catherine of Aragon, Anne Boleyn, Jane Seymour, Anne of Cleves, Catherine Howard and Katherine Parr.

The English Reformation

In the 1530s, Henry VIII broke away from the Roman Catholic Church and set himself up as the Supreme Head of the new Church of England.

Defender of the Faith

Henry VIII was a loyal Catholic who was deeply hostile to the ideas of church reform that swept through Europe in the 1520s. He even published a defence of Catholic traditions, earning himself the title of Defender of the Faith in 1521. However, Henry grew angry when the Pope, the head of the Catholic Church, refused to annul his marriage to Catherine of Aragon. In the 1530s, Henry took control of the Church in England. Now he, not the Pope, would appoint church leaders.

In Germany, a monk called Martin Luther led a rebellion against the wealth and privilege of the Catholic Church. In 1520 he publicly burned a written warning from the Pope in the streets of Wittenberg.

In this era, known as the Reformation, it was an act of treason to disobey Henry's new Church of England. He abolished the Catholic monasteries and confiscated their wealth and lands. An official Bible in English was published in 1539. In the short reign of Henry's son, Edward VI (1547–53), the English Church became more Protestant. Catholic practices, such as church decoration and the feasts of saints, were done away with. English was used in church services instead of Latin. England was now a Protestant land.

Ireland, 1534–41

In 1537, the Irish Parliament recognized Henry's position as Head of the Irish Church and the Irish monasteries were dissolved. Four years later, the Dublin Parliament agreed to Henry's new title of King of Ireland. However, the bulk of the Irish population remained Catholic and the Reformation put down only shallow roots in Ireland.

Wales, 1534–51

The Welsh clergy swore oaths of loyalty to the English king and many Catholic monks found new posts as parish priests in the new church. The compulsory use of the English Prayer Book posed a serious threat to the Welsh language, but William Salesbury made unofficial translations of the Gospels and Prayer Book. Thanks to these and later official translations, Welsh became a printed language. Between 1536 and 1543, a series of acts tied Wales more closely to the English system of government.

Scotland, 1528–60

Scotland was split by these religious changes. Scots who wanted church reform looked to Protestant England for help. Catholic Scots were pleased when their infant queen married a French Catholic prince. Until 1560, French governors and French troops controlled the important posts in Scotland. Many Scots, however, were horrified by the persecution of church reformers by the Catholic authorities, especially the burning of an 83-year-old priest. After 1558 they hoped that Elizabeth, the new Protestant Queen of England, would help bring about change. In 1559, Protestant preachers encouraged mobs to 'cleanse' churches of Catholic objects. English troops landed at the important port of Leith near Edinburgh and the Scottish Parliament passed laws that turned Scotland into a Protestant nation.

Timeline

1521	• Henry VIII is made Defender of the Faith by Pope Leo X
1534	• Refusal to acknowledge Henry as Head of the Church made a treasonable offence
1536	• Smaller English monasteries brought under royal control and dissolved
1539	• Publication of the official Great Bible in English
1539	• Remaining monasteries in England and Wales dissolved
1541	• Kingdom of Ireland established
1549	• Protestant *Book of Common Prayer* introduced into English churches
1558	• Protestant Elizabeth becomes Queen of England
1560	• French troops withdraw from Scotland
1560	• Scottish Parliament passes laws to abolish the old Church
1567	• First translation of the Bible into Welsh

Protestant ideas spread quickly throughout Scotland. The reformer John Knox preached against the 'sinful' worship of images in the Catholic Church.

The Regiment of Women

In an age when men were expected to govern, three women ruled parts of Britain as queen. But they faced serious problems caused by the Reformation.

'Bloody Mary'

Although she was a devout Catholic, Henry VIII's eldest daughter, Mary Tudor, was quietly accepted as queen by most of her English subjects in 1553. Mary had two aims: to restore the Catholic Church and to produce a Catholic heir. Almost 300 Protestant 'heretics', including Thomas Cranmer, the Archbishop of Canterbury, were burned at the stake. In 1554 Mary married the Catholic Philip of Spain, but they had no children. In 1558, Mary supported Spain in a war against France, but lost Calais, the last English possession in France. When Mary died at the early age of forty-two, Protestant England rejoiced.

Mary Tudor arrives in London in 1553 as the new Queen of England. Her half-sister, Elizabeth, stands behind her.

Mary of Scotland

The Catholic princess, Mary Stewart, returned from France to rule Protestant Scotland in 1561. Mary's reign began well. She was attractive, intelligent, well educated and took care not to anger her Protestant subjects. Mary's hold on power seemed secure, but her need to produce an heir led to her downfall. When she married the Catholic nobleman, Henry Darnley, Scottish Protestants were concerned that this would result in a new line of Catholic monarchs. Support for Mary quickly evaporated. Then Darnley died in mysterious circumstances, in an explosion thought to be the work of Lord Bothwell. When Mary subsequently married Bothwell, the nobility were outraged. Mary was forced to abdicate and was imprisoned in the island fortress of Lochleven. She escaped and fled to England, hoping for protection from her half-sister, Elizabeth. Instead she suffered a further nineteen years in prison. After rumours of Catholic plots to put Mary on the English throne, Elizabeth ordered her execution. Mary Queen of Scots was beheaded at Fotheringay in 1587.

Timeline	
1553	• Catholic Mary I inherits the English throne
1554	• Mary weds Philip of Spain
1555-8	• Mary persecutes English Protestants
1558	• Calais, the last English possession in France, is lost
1558	• Death of Mary I
1558	• Protestant Elizabeth I inherits the English throne
1561	• Mary Stewart inherits the Scottish throne
1565	• Mary of Scotland marries Henry Darnley
1567	• Mary loses control of Scotland and is forced to abdicate
1587	• Mary is executed at Fotheringay Castle

Elizabeth of England

When young, the Protestant Princess Elizabeth had almost been executed because of her religious beliefs. When she became queen she wanted peace between her Protestant and Catholic subjects. As long as they outwardly obeyed the Church of England, she did not 'make windows into men's souls'. Her long reign of forty-four years gave the people of England time to get used to Protestant ways of worship. By the end of her reign, only her most elderly subjects could remember the old Catholic Church.

'Gloriana'

Elizabeth saw the problems the two Marys had faced and decided not to marry. Instead she encouraged the idea that she was a selfless monarch who put the needs of her people before her own happiness as a woman. She travelled round England on lengthy progresses, or tours, so that her subjects could see her in all her majesty. The arts of architecture, music and drama were used in elaborate ceremonies and processions that celebrated Elizabeth's reign as 'Queen Gloriana'.

Elizabeth I, known as the 'virgin queen', ruled England for forty-four years.

The Union of the Crowns

A wedding in Edinburgh, Scotland, in 1503 joined together the Houses of Tudor and Stewart. Gradually the ancient enemies of Scotland and England began to merge into a united Britain.

Following the death of her first husband in 1560, Mary Stewart married Lord Darnley, below, with whom she had a son.

The Thistle and the Rose

In 1503, James IV of Scotland married the English princess, Margaret Tudor, at Holyrood Abbey. Margaret's father, Henry VII, wanted peace on England's northern border. This 'union of the thistle [Scotland] and the rose [England]' kept the peace for a while. However, when war broke out between France and England in 1513, James supported the French and died in battle at Flodden. He left a son, James V, who carried Stewart and Tudor blood in his veins. The Scottish kings now had a strong claim to the thrones of both kingdoms.

The Plans of Henry VIII

In 1543, Henry VIII wanted the Scottish nobles to agree to a marriage between the infant Mary of Scotland and the Prince of Wales. After the marriage, Henry meant to keep Mary in England and govern Scotland himself. However, the Scottish Parliament threw out the marriage plans. In 1544, Henry's war fleet attacked the Forth valley. Even Holyrood Palace, built by James IV for his English wife, was destroyed. The invasion was repeated the following year. But the Scots resisted Henry, and his plans to merge the two kingdoms failed.

Timeline	
1503	• Marriage of James IV to Margaret Tudor
1513	• Death of James IV at Flodden Field
1543	• Henry VIII tries to take charge of Scotland
1544	• English raids on Scotland
1567	• Birth in Edinburgh of James Stewart, first King of Great Britain
1586	• In the Treaty of Berwick, James promises to help England
1603	• James VI of Scotland crowned as James I of England
1604	• James styles himself as King of Great Britain

The Protestant King

The Scottish King James VI was Protestant and had a good claim to the English throne. In 1586 he promised to support England if it was attacked by Catholic France or Spain. He made little protest when his Catholic mother was executed in 1587. The childless Elizabeth I paid a generous annual pension to James throughout the last seventeen years of her reign. After Elizabeth's death in March 1603, James was declared as King of England.

Two Kingdoms

James styled himself King of Great Britain and approved the design of a union flag that combined the crosses of the Scottish St Andrew and the English St George. However, although they had the same king, the two kingdoms were not unified. Their Parliaments, Churches and laws remained separate. James greatly enjoyed the increased authority and wealth that flowed from his new status in London. He governed Scotland through a few loyal men and only returned there once, in 1617.

Foiling the 'Popish plot': in this artist's impression of events, Guy Fawkes is caught red-handed with barrels of gunpowder in the cellars of the Palace of Westminster.

The Gunpowder Plot

After 1603, English Catholics were fearful of the Protestant king from Scotland. Some Catholics devised plots to assassinate him. The most famous of these was the Gunpowder Plot of 1605, where conspirators plotted to blow up the Palace of Westminster while the king and the Protestant nobility attended the opening of Parliament. Catholics had been suspected of disloyalty since the Reformation. After 1605, the celebration of the plot's failure every 5 November linked Catholicism with treason in the Protestant public's mind.

King and Parliament

After 1530, Parliament became an important part of English government and a powerful partner to the Tudor Crown. However, the Stewart monarchs had a more difficult relationship with Parliament.

The Tudor Parliament

In the 1530s, Parliament emerged as a national institution. Henry VIII needed it to support his Reformation of the Church and to agree to his new role as Supreme Head of the Church. Henry wanted his new laws to be passed by the king, House of Lords and House of Commons acting together. Edward VI and Mary I also used Parliament to bring about important religious changes. It became an important point of contact between the government and the governed, especially as the Commons grew in size and influence. However, Parliament did not have a clear place in the government of England. It did not meet every year, and for long periods when Elizabeth was on the English throne it did not meet at all.

Parliament and the Stewarts

James I disliked the control the London Parliament had over his income. For its part, Parliament disliked James' extravagance with money and his belief that God had given him the right to govern as he pleased. James dissolved angry Parliaments in 1611 and 1612. In 1621, Parliament even accused the king's Lord Chancellor, Francis Bacon, of corruption. Friction between King and Parliament increased under Charles I, who shared his father James's belief in the divine right of kings to govern. Charles was also suspected of being a secret Catholic and of seeking to gain absolute power. He was angered by Parliament's unwillingness to allow him the money he needed for his wars in Europe. Before its dissolution in 1629, Parliament drew up a petition of rights. This stated the freedoms of

This contemporary engraving shows a meeting of the House of Lords under King Henry VIII, with the Commons in attendance.

Englishmen under the law and aimed to limit abuses of royal power such as interference with subjects' property and illegal arrest. Charles responded by governing for the next eleven years without once calling Parliament. This had been common enough in earlier ages, but by the mid-17th century many people viewed Charles' personal rule as a tyranny. His levying of old taxes, such as ship money, only added to the growing discontent throughout England.

The scientist and philosopher, Francis Bacon, served as Lord Chancellor to James I but was sent to the Tower of London and fined a huge amount of money after parliamentary committees found him guilty of corruption.

The Scottish Parliament

The Scottish Parliament grew out of the medieval royal council. It met to agree taxes, but also influenced justice, foreign policy and even education. The Scottish Parliament had little real power at this time, but it could cause problems for unpopular kings such as James III. Unlike the English Parliament, the lords and the commoners of Scotland sat together and debated in the same Parliament Hall. In the 1630s, a beautiful new Parliament building was built in Edinburgh.

Timeline

1530s	• Henry VIII uses Parliament to show national support for his religious changes in England
1611-12	• James I clashes with the English Parliament over royal debts and powers
1620s	• The House of Commons grows in authority and confidence to challenge the king
1628	• The Commons attempts to limit royal power in a petition of rights
1629-40	• Charles I rules without calling Parliament
1630s	• Scottish Parliament Hall built in Edinburgh

The War of Three Kingdoms

A national revolt in Scotland led to civil war in all parts of Britain and Ireland. The war ended with the execution of the king.

Charles I, shown here out hunting, believed he could rule England without using Parliament. He tried to quash opposition but his actions led to the outbreak of civil war in Scotland, England and Ireland.

Revolution in Scotland

In 1637, Charles I tried to make the Scottish Kirk, or national church, more like the Church of England. This caused riots in Edinburgh. The Scots drew up a national covenant and opposed the king. Charles tried to force the Scots to obey him, but his army was defeated and he had to agree to pay them a grant of £300,000. To raise this money, Charles was forced to recall England's Parliament in 1640.

The Long Parliament

Charles's heavy-handed policies and overspending had made him deeply unpopular with Parliament. It passed acts to limit the king's powers. In one of them, Parliament forbade its dissolution without its own consent and decreed that it should meet more regularly. A Catholic uprising in Ireland brought the crisis to a head. Parliamentary leaders did not trust the king with the army that would be raised to re-conquer Ireland. But Charles believed it was his right as king to command the army. In January 1642, Charles entered Parliament with soldiers and tried to arrest his opponents. This action lost Charles even more support and England drifted towards civil war.

King Against Parliament

The royalists (king's supporters) narrowly won the first battle of the war at Edgehill in 1642, but failed to march on London. Parliament, helped by the Scots, won a clear victory at Marston Moor in 1644. Without access to the major ports, Charles was slowly drained of resources. He could still raise troops in the West Country and Highland Scotland, but they lacked weapons and supplies. Parliament controlled the south of England, where towns and industry were concentrated, and successfully raised and trained its well-equipped New Model Army. At Naseby, in 1645, Charles could only muster 7,000 men against a 'roundhead' army twice the size. With his realm reduced to a few isolated strongholds, Charles surrendered to the Scots at Newark in 1646.

Towards the Scaffold

Despite the war between Charles and his subjects, many people in Scotland, England and Ireland still felt a sense of loyalty to the king, but Charles was about to test this loyalty to the limit. When he tried to re-start the war in 1648, it was easier for his enemies to present him as untrustworthy and as an obstacle to peace. Charles was tried for treason and executed at Whitehall, London, in January 1649. About one in four of the English male population had fought in the wars and around 200,000 Englishmen had died in combat or from disease. In Scotland and Ireland, rich cities like Aberdeen had been brutally sacked.

Charles showed great personal courage at his execution in January 1649. Royalist supporters later created a cult of martyrdom around his memory.

Timeline

1638	• Scots sign a national covenant in defence of their liberties
1639-40	• Charles defeated by the Scots and forced to recall the English Parliament
1640	• The Long Parliament clashes with the king and his ministers
1641	• Catholic uprising in Ireland raises fear of royal tyranny
1642	• First battle between royal and parliamentary forces at Edgehill
1644	• Scots and parliamentary armies defeat Charles at Marston Moor near York
1645	• Charles loses Battle of Naseby in Northamptonshire
1648	• Charles tries to fight a second war in England
1649	• Charles found guilty of high treason and executed at Whitehall

The Age of Cromwell

With the army behind him, the politician Oliver Cromwell rose to power in England. In the 1640s and 1650s he came close to uniting Britain by force by invading parts of Scotland and Ireland.

God's Englishman

Oliver Cromwell was a landowner and Member of Parliament who recruited a cavalry troop in 1642 and fought at Edgehill and Marston Moor. By 1645 he had risen to high command in Parliament's New Model Army. When Charles tried to re-start the war in 1648, Cromwell emerged as a political leader. He defeated the royalist forces in Wales then marched north to defeat a Scottish army, now supporting Charles, at Preston. Cromwell grew increasingly irritated by the squabbling in Parliament and the king's scheming. He came to believe that Charles should be brought to trial and he served in the court that tried the king and signed his death warrant. A Commonwealth of England, or republic, was declared in May 1649.

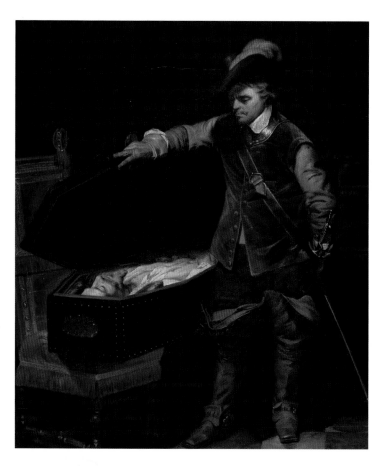

The politician Oliver Cromwell regards the corpse of Charles I, whose death warrant he signed.

Cromwell in Ireland

During a bloody nine-month campaign in 1649–50, Cromwell conquered much of eastern Ireland, taking the key ports of Wexford and Drogheda. The re-conquest of Ireland was especially brutal. Many of Cromwell's troops were Protestants who hated Catholics and remembered the atrocities carried out by Irish Catholics against Protestants in 1641. There were terrible massacres at Wexford and Drogheda, and many Irish people were butchered or rounded up and sold into slavery in the West Indies.

In December 1653, Cromwell took control of Parliament and was made Lord Protector of England, gaining the powers of a king.

The Invasion of Scotland

Many Scots nobles still supported the Stewarts, so in 1650 Cromwell marched north, defeated a Scots army at Dunbar and entered Edinburgh. Despite this, Charles II was crowned King of Scots at Scone near Perth in early 1651, but few Scots rallied to the new king and his army was defeated at Worcester in September. Cromwell was now master of both kingdoms and set about uniting them into one state. Lowland Scotland was garrisoned and the Highlands were sealed off by a chain of forts. Royalist risings there in 1653 and 1654 were crushed. Cromwell's rule was unpopular, but as the Kirk was untouched, it went largely unopposed.

The Protectorate

After 1650 the London Parliament was weakened by infighting and failed to govern the country effectively. In December 1653, Cromwell took power as Lord Protector. His division of England into fifteen military districts was unpopular. The local commissioners or government officials were mostly Puritans who used their powers to force the population to behave in 'godly ways'. Cromwell introduced civil marriages and allowed Jews to settle and live in England, but these changes offended many traditionally minded people. By the time Cromwell fell ill and died in 1658, England had become tired of the republican experiment.

Timeline

1647	• Cromwell rises to the rank of lieutenant general of the parliamentary cavalry
1648	• Cromwell defeats royalist uprisings in Pembroke and at Preston
1649-50	• Cromwell commands the parliamentary forces in Ireland
1649	• Cromwell signs death warrant of Charles I
1650-52	• Cromwell invades Scotland and imposes union with England
1653	• On 15 December, Cromwell is sworn in as Lord Protector
1654-7	• Jews are permitted to return to England
1657	• Cromwell is offered the Crown by Parliament but refuses to accept it
1658	• Cromwell dies suddenly in September from 'malarial fever'
1661	• Cromwell's body is dug up from Westminster Abbey and hung on the gallows at Tyburn, London

The Restoration

In 1660, Charles II returned from exile and the Puritan Commonwealth came to an end. There were few protests and many welcomed the return of a prince who would come to be known as 'the merry monarch'.

The End of the Republic

With Cromwell dead, England seemed on the brink of chaos. General Monck arrived in London with his well disciplined troops in time to keep order. A new moderate Parliament met and Charles II was invited to return from exile. There were few demonstrations in support of the Commonwealth. Most Englishmen were tired of political disputes and the strict Puritan religion. Charles II did not take a heavy revenge on his enemies. He was a flexible politician who understood the importance of bringing peace to his tired kingdom. Cromwell's corpse was dug up and abused, but most of the leading

On 29 May 1660, Charles II returned to London, marking the end of the Commonwealth and the restoration of royal rule in Britain.

Timeline

1660	• Monarchy under Charles II restored by Parliament
1662	• Parliament passes the strict Act of Uniformity
1665	• Bubonic plague kills approximately 80,000 Londoners
1666	• The Great Fire of London rages from 2-5 September
1670s	• Catholics are excluded from official posts by the Test Acts
1685	• Death of Charles II

parliamentarians were pardoned. Only the 'regicides', who had executed Charles' father in 1649, were severely punished. Charles made it clear to all that he was happy to govern in partnership with Parliament. The king was granted sufficient privileges and money by Parliament, but Parliament was also careful to ensure that he did not have so much that he tried to rule too independently, like his father.

The Restoration in Ireland and Scotland

After the Cromwellian conquest, large parts of Ireland were taken from Catholic landowners and given to Protestants. The original owners struggled to regain their land after 1660. In Scotland, Charles introduced changes to the Kirk in 1662 that outraged over 300 ministers. They began to preach to their congregations in outdoor services called 'conventicles'. Government troops were used to stop these illegal prayer meetings. This led to fierce popular resistance by the Covenanters, especially in south-western Scotland.

Religious Troubles in England

Charles tolerated members of other churches, but the Parliament elected in 1661 was determined to enforce strict obedience to Anglican ways of worship. The 1662 Act of Uniformity forced 2,000 moderate Presbyterians to conform to or quit the Church of England. The Test Acts of the 1670s also excluded Catholics and 'nonconforming' Protestants from government office.

The Merry Monarch?

The Great Plague of 1665 and the Great Fire of London in 1666 cast a shadow over the early years of Charles' reign. War with the Dutch and religious conflict in Scotland added to his problems. Nevertheless, the restored king generally governed 'lightly' and worked with Parliament.

The Great Fire

In September 1666, the medieval city of London was destroyed by fire that lasted four days. The old cathedral of St Paul's and 87 parish churches were destroyed, as were over 13,000 houses. Although few deaths were recorded, most of the 80,000 inhabitants of the city area were left homeless.

The Great Fire of London is said to have started in a bakery in Pudding Lane. A brisk east wind made the flames leap and helped carry the blaze quickly across the city.

The Glorious Revolution

In 1688 the last Catholic King of Great Britain was overthrown and replaced by Protestant monarchs who promised to uphold the rights of Parliament.

The Last Catholic King

In 1685, the Catholic James succeeded his brother Charles and became king. In England, Parliament grew uneasy at the increase in James's army and concerned that his senior officers were Catholic. James also favoured Catholics for important royal posts. The final straw was the birth of a male heir in June 1688. The infant James would be raised a Catholic. The Protestant fear of a line of Catholic rulers seemed to be coming true. They had only to look to France, where Louis XIV was persecuting his Protestant subjects, to see their own likely fate.

Timeline

June 1688	• English nobles invite William of Orange to intervene on behalf of the Protestant cause
5 November 1688	• William lands at Brixham near Torquay in Devon
10 December 1688	• After defeat at Reading, James's forces melt away
23 December 1688	• James is allowed to flee to France
February 1689	• William and Mary become King and Queen of England
April 1689	• Scottish Parliament chooses William as its sovereign
July 1690	• William defeats James at the Battle of the Boyne near Drogheda

The fleet of the Dutch prince, the Protestant William of Orange, sets out on its journey to England from the Netherlands in 1688.

The 'Bloodless Revolution'

Protestant hopes centred upon the Dutch prince, William of Orange, a Protestant and the husband of the Protestant princess, Mary Stewart. In November 1688, William's fleet crossed the English Channel. Flying banners in support of 'English liberties and the Protestant religion', he received a warm welcome on landing in Devon. Nobles throughout England soon declared support for William. After losing the first skirmish, James disbanded his army and was allowed to slip away to exile in France. Parliament ruled that, by fleeing the realm, James had abdicated. William and Mary were invited to reign together in England. A bill of rights limited the powers of the monarch and confirmed Parliament's place at the heart of English government. The succession was also settled. Protestant Anne would rule after William and Mary. Catholics were barred from the English throne.

Civil War

The revolution was not bloodless in Scotland where many Scots remained loyal to the Stewarts. These men had sworn oaths to James, who came from a royal house that had ruled Scotland for 400 years. When the Parliament met in Edinburgh in 1689, the city was full of armed supporters of the opposing Stewart and Orange causes. The Parliament selected William and Mary as their new monarchs because William could be trusted to defend the Presbyterian Kirk. Supporters of the Stewarts rode out of Edinburgh to gather their forces. These 'Jacobites' slaughtered a government army at Killiecrankie in Perthshire later that summer, and the Jacobite threat would haunt Scotland for decades.

Battle of the Boyne

James' strongest support came from Catholic Ireland. He was greeted warmly when he landed at Dublin in 1689 at the head of 6,000 French troops. In 1690, James and William met in battle along the River Boyne near Drogheda. The battle was indecisive, but the disheartened James returned to France.

Almost 60,000 men fought at the Battle of the Boyne, where James' cavalry was ranged against William's disciplined army.

21

Tudor and Stewart Ireland

English and then British monarchs encouraged Protestants from Britain to settle in Ireland. There were many settlers in the northern province of Ulster. Their presence inspired resistance from the Irish people already living there.

The First Plantations

In the 1550s, Edward VI and his sister Mary began to settle English colonists in Ireland. These 'plantations' were meant to extend English rule deep into the heart of Ireland, but the Irish resisted fiercely over the next twenty years. Elizabeth I also tried and failed to plant English colonists in Ulster in 1570. When rebellion erupted in Ireland in the 1590s, the English colonists in the province of Munster had to abandon their farms and shelter from the Irish in walled towns.

A map showing England, Ireland and Wales in the late 1500s. It shows us that while map-makers were familiar with the shape of Britain, Ireland was still a distant and little known land.

The Nine Years' War, 1594–1603

As they were Catholic, the Irish and Anglo-Irish lords played little part in the royal government in Dublin. When Hugh O'Neill, the Earl of Tyrone rebelled in 1594, his army contained many of the Catholic Irish ruling class who were angry that they were not allowed to hold government posts. Tyrone's men were well equipped and highly experienced soldiers who defeated three English armies between 1595 and 1600. New armies from England eventually forced O'Neill to surrender in 1603. He was allowed to keep his lands, but left Ireland with his supporters four years later when English law was imposed upon Ulster. For the first time, London could claim to control the whole of Ireland.

Confcientia mille teftes

The Ulster Plantation

In 1603, James VI of Scotland also became King of Ireland. After the departure of the O'Neills, four million acres of their land in Ulster was taken over by the Crown. James revived the policy of plantation, but on a much greater scale than before. Protestant landowners were banned from renting land to Irish tenants or from selling land to a Gael. The new farmers of Ulster were from James' British kingdoms and were Protestant. James was keen that the Ulster plantation should be a joint British settlement, so half of the colonists were Scots.

The Impact of Plantation

By 1630, there were over 80,000 British Protestant settlers in the six counties of Ulster. The settlers in Ulster and in the later colonies at Wexford and Munster set about transforming the economy and landscape of Ireland. The old ways of herding that had been followed by the Gaelic clans gave way to the more profitable growing of crops. Forests were cut down for building and shipping and much of the bog-land was drained. The old tribal townships were replaced by larger planned towns on the English model. The Catholics were not supposed to rent farmland, but many carried on as tenant farmers if only because skilled labour remained scarce.

Faced with overwhelming odds, the Earl of Tyrone was forced to surrender in 1603.

Timeline

1556	• First English plantations founded in Laois and Offaly in mid-Ireland
1570	• Elizabethan plantations in Ulster
1594	• The O'Neill clan rises up against English rule
1595	• The English are defeated at Clontibret
1598	• O'Neill wins a major victory at Yellow Ford
1603	• Irish forces under O'Neill surrender after siege of Kinsale
1607	• O'Neill sails into exile in Catholic Europe
1603	• Extensive Protestant plantations in Ulster

Exploration and Trade

England played an important part in the growth of European trade after 1500. British explorers founded trading posts and then colonies in far-flung lands.

Sir Walter Raleigh founded the first English colony in the New World in 1585.

Northern Explorers

In 1497, the Italian navigator Giovanni Caboto sailed on the Bristol ship *Matthew* to 'a new founde land' in the far west, where the ocean teemed with cod. Later explorers returned to northern America looking for a north-west passage to the Pacific. In the 1570s, Martin Frobisher made three expeditions to the far north of Canada, but these dangerous journeys yielded little more than valueless ores. In the 1550s, Bristol-born Richard Chancellor travelled twice to northern Russia.

English America

In the 1580s, Walter Raleigh organized three expeditions to North America. But his settlement at Roanoke Island off North Carolina lacked supplies and the starving colonists were evacuated in 1586. Other more successful English colonies followed at Jamestown in Virginia in 1608, in Massachusetts in 1620 and at Maryland in 1634. By 1700, more than 200,000 settlers from Britain and Ireland had emigrated to North America. However, England's richest possessions were the West Indies, where sugar agriculture began in the 1630s. By 1672, a settlement at another Jamestown, near Accra in West Africa, gave the English an important slice of the Atlantic slave trade.

Timeline

1497	• Giovanni Caboto sails from Bristol to Newfoundland
1554-6	• Richard Chancellor travels to Muscovy, Russia
1576-8	• Frobisher explores the coastline of northern Canada
1585	• English colony established on Roanoke Island in Virginia
1600	• Charter granted to the East India Company
1608	• Jamestown settlement founded in Virginia
1620	• English settlers land at Plymouth, Massachusetts
1627	• Scottish settlement founded in Nova Scotia
1670	• East India Company given important rights by Charles II
1672	• English slave merchants control Jamestown near Accra

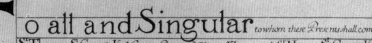

The East India Company

The London East India Company was set up in 1600 to challenge the Dutch-Portuguese monopoly of the spice trade. At first the company struggled to gain a foothold, but it gradually established trading posts in Madras, Bombay and Calcutta. By the end of the century there were more than thirty English trading posts in India, dealing in silks, dyes and tea. The company's navy gave it access to the eastern spice trade and helped it establish a base in China by 1712. In 1670, Charles II gave the company the right to raise troops, mint currency, form alliances and hold courts in its areas of influence. By the early 1700s, the company operated as an independent kingdom within India, making great fortunes for its shareholders and employees alike.

A series of acts under Charles II gave the East India Company rights that had previously been reserved for monarchs.

Scottish Expansion

In 1621, Sir William Alexander was granted a charter to found a Scottish colony in North America. After difficulties, Nova Scotia (New Scotland) was established in 1627, but it was abandoned in the 1630s when Charles I gave the colony to France. The main direction of Scottish expansion of trade was eastwards to Europe. Campveere in the Netherlands became the port of entry for all Scottish trade in 1541. Other Scots merchants went further east into the Baltic, and by 1600 there were Scottish trading posts in Danzig, Cracow and Konigsberg. Companies of Scottish soldiers also went into service as mercenaries in the armies of Swedish, Polish and Russian rulers.

The Kingdom of Great Britain

The Kingdom of Great Britain came into being in 1707. The Treaty of Union merged England and Scotland, two ancient kingdoms with a long history of distrust and dislike, but also with much in common.

The Catholic claimant to the English and Scottish thrones, James Francis Edward Stewart. His faith made him unacceptable to the largely Protestant population of Britain.

The Act of Settlement

Queen Anne was the last Protestant Stewart monarch and she had no living children. The exiled Prince James Francis Edward Stewart had the strongest claim to the English and Scottish thrones, but as a Catholic he was unacceptable. In the 1701 Act of Settlement, the English Parliament decided that on Anne's death the English Crown would pass to the Protestant rulers of the German principality of Hanover. This deeply angered the Scots, who had not been consulted. The Scottish Parliament stated it would choose its own monarch, but the English feared a Catholic Stewart upon the Scottish throne and a French invasion by the 'back door' (in other words, through Scotland). Parliament in London said the Scots must enter into negotiations for a full union with England by Christmas Day 1705, or they and their goods would be considered alien. Facing the destruction of their trade with England, the Scottish Parliament agreed to negotiate with London.

Full Union

In 1706, thirty-one representatives from England and Scotland gathered in secret in Whitehall to agree the terms of union. Despite riots and a flood of anti-union petitions, the Scottish Parliament finally accepted the treaty in January 1707. In England, the union was celebrated with gun salutes at the Tower of London, for it seemed that the Catholic threat had been defeated. The treaty was not popular north of the border, however, where it meant the abolition of the Scottish Parliament. The Scots only received sixty-one seats out of a total of 709 in the new British Houses of Parliament. They also lost their currency, but were allowed to trade with England's colonies overseas and permitted to keep their own laws and their Kirk.

'A Treaty Unravelled'

Many Scots soon regretted the union. In London, new laws were passed that were in breach of the treaty. The London Parliament also gave rights to those who used English forms of worship in Scotland. Many Scots objected to this interference in Scottish life. They also resented having to pay higher taxes to fund England's wars in Europe. Scotland's trade with its old ally, France, declined and this led to a rise in smuggling. By 1713, many Scottish nobles, merchants and churchmen were deeply unhappy with the union. A crisis came when the government proposed a new tax on malt, again a breach of the treaty. A bill to repeal the union was brought in and defeated by only four votes in the Lords. For the Scots, at least, the union had got off to a bad start.

Timeline

1701	• English Act of Settlement ensures that the throne passes to Protestants
1703-4	• Scottish Parliament asserts its independence from England
1705	• Aliens Act threatens Scots with trade penalties
1706	• Commissioners from both parliaments meet in Whitehall
1707	• Treaty of Union between Scotland and England
1707	• Establishment of the United Kingdom
1709	• English Treason Act extended to Scotland
1711	• Toleration extended to Church of England worshippers in Scotland
1713	• Bill to repeal the union fails by four votes
1715-60	• Serious decline in Scottish economy

The Duke of Queensbury presents the Treaty of Union to Queen Anne in London in May 1707.

The Jacobite Risings

To the Jacobites, the true king was James Stewart and the Treaty of Union was an agreement signed by an illegal monarch and rebel parliaments.

Bonnie Prince Charlie (seated) meets Flora MacDonald, the Jacobite heroine who sheltered him during his campaign.

The 1715 Rising

On his arrival from Hanover in 1714, the new King George I sacked Anne's old ministers. One of these angry and disappointed men was the Earl of Mar. He took up the Jacobite cause at Braemar in the eastern Highlands in 1715 and quickly gathered an impressive army of 12,000 men. However, government forces blocked Mar at the Battle of Sheriffmuir near Stirling. Unable to break out of the Highlands, Mar could not link up with the Jacobites in northern England. By the time James Francis Edward Stewart arrived from France in December, the rising was already over.

The 1745 Rising

In July 1745, James' son, Charles Edward Stewart, sailed to Scotland and landed in the Hebrides with only seven companions. The clans had not forgotten the disappointment of 1715 and the risk of failure was high. Nevertheless, by late September 'Bonnie Prince Charlie' had gathered an army, captured Perth, defeated the government forces in Scotland at Prestonpans and was holding court in his ancestors' palace of Holyrood. With winter closing in, Charles struck out southwards, reaching Derby, a mere 208 km (129 miles) from London, in early December. There was panic in London and the belongings of the royal Hanoverians were flung onto

The British army outnumbered and outgunned the Jacobites at the Battle of Culloden in 1746.

Thames barges as they prepared to flee the city. However, the exhausted Jacobites turned homeward. They won a further victory at Falkirk in January, but were pushed northwards by the advance of larger Hanoverian forces. On the flat Culloden Moor near Inverness, the Jacobites were easily cut down by government troops.

After Culloden

The Jacobite threat was over, but the London government made a great effort to clamp down on the Highlands. The clans were disarmed and the chiefs lost their old powers. Tartan and the bagpipes were banned. In 1748, the Hanoverian government began building its final solution to the Highland problem. Fort George near Inverness took over twenty years to complete and cost the vast sum of £200,000 (more than a billion pounds today). Holding over 2,000 troops and 3,000 barrels of gunpowder, it was the largest fortification built in 18th-century Europe. It reminds us of the terror that the Jacobite Highlanders inspired in southern Britain.

Britain in 1750

Culloden was the last major battle fought on British soil. After 1750, Scotland and England were at peace. For over 200 years, the religion of the monarch had been very important in British politics. That age was over, because from now on real power in Britain would increasingly be held by Parliament and the Prime Minister.

Defensive structures such as Fort George were crucial in suppressing local resistance and maintaining order.

Timeline

1714	• Queen Anne succeeded by George of Hanover
1715	• Mar unable to break out of Highlands after Battle of Sheriffmuir
August 1745	• Bonnie Prince Charlie lands in the western Highlands
September 1745	• Government army in Scotland defeated at Prestonpans
December 1745	• Charles' army reaches Derby, causing panic in London
January 1746	• Jacobites win their last victory at Falkirk
April 1746	• Jacobites badly defeated at Culloden near Inverness
1748	• Government begins building massive forts at Fort George

Glossary

abdicate to give up one's kingdom

Anglican someone or something to do with the Church of England

annul to announce that something, for example a marriage, no longer exists

Catholic to do with the Roman Catholic form of Christianity

cavalry soldiers on horseback

charter a formal statement of rights

civil war a war fought by different groups of people living in the same country

clan a Gaelic name for a family or network of families

colonist someone who goes to live in a colony (see below)

colony a territory owned by another country, usually for trading

commissioner a member of the old Scottish Parliament or a burgh (area) council

conspirator someone who plots with other people to do something

covenant a solemn or sacred agreement

Covenanters people who supported the reformed Protestant Church of Scotland

dissolve to end or close a Parliament

divine right a privilege believed to be given by God

foundries workshops where metals are worked into tools and weapons

Gaels the Celtic peoples of Ireland and the Scottish Highlands

garrison to occupy a town with troops

heretic someone accused of and often punished for belonging to a different faith

Jacobite a supporter of the Stewart royal family

Kirk the reformed Protestant Church of Scotland

levy to impose a tax on people

malt an important ingredient in making beer and whisky

mercenaries soldiers who fight for any country or group that pays them

monopoly to have complete control of something, so that others have no share

New Model Army the best known of the Parliamentarian armies in the English civil war, comprising professional soldiers led by trained generals

ore rock containing small pieces of metal

plantations groups of settlers

Pope leader of the Roman Catholic Church

Protestant a supporter of the reformed Christian churches after 1530

Puritan someone, usually Protestant, who lives a strictly religious life

Reformation a religious and political movement of 16th-century Europe

regicide a person who kills a king, or the act of killing a king

repeal to reverse a law so that it no longer has any legal force

republican describes a country without a king or queen, governed by representatives of the people

roundhead a supporter of the English Parliament against Charles I

shareholder someone who owns part (shares) in a company

tyranny unlimited power that is used unfairly and cruelly

Ulster a province of Northern Ireland that was given to English and Scottish Protestant settlers in the 17th century

Timeline

1503	• James IV of Scotland marries Margaret Tudor
1533	• Henry VIII begins the Reformation in England
1536	• Smaller English monasteries abolished
1536-42	• Wales brought more fully under English legal system
1558	• The Protestant Elizabeth succeeds her Catholic sister, Mary
1587	• Execution of Mary of Scotland
1603	• James VI of Scotland inherits England
1604	• James VI begins to 'plant' settlers in Ulster
1605	• Gunpowder plot to blow up Parliament fails
1608	• English colony at Jamestown in Virginia established
1637	• National rebellion against Charles I begins in Edinburgh
1642	• First major battle of the civil war in England at Edgehill
1649	• Charles I executed at Whitehall in London
1653	• Cromwell becomes Lord Protector of England
1660	• Restoration of the monarchy under Charles II
1688	• James II and VII deposed by William of Orange
1690	• James loses at the Battle of the Boyne in Ireland
1701	• English Crown settled on the House of Hanover
1707	• Treaty of Union forms the United Kingdom
1715	• Jacobite Rising under the Earl of Mar
1745-46	• Bonnie Prince Charlie tries to win back thrones for the Stewarts

Further Information

Books

Rediscovering the Making of the United Kingdom, Colin Shephard and Tim Lomas, Hodder, 2001

On the Trail of the Tudors, Richard Wood, Franklin Watts, 2000

History From Buildings: Tudor Britain, Stewart Ross, Franklin Watts, 2006

Scotland in the Early Modern Age, Richard Dargie, Pulse Publications, 2005

Britain in Tudor Times, Fiona MacDonald, Franklin Watts, 2003

An Introduction to Stuart Britain, 1603–1714, Hodder Murray, 1999

Websites

www.britainexpress.com/History/
clearly written introductions to key topics, such as main characters and events

www.royal.gov.uk/
authoritative accounts of the lives of all the Tudor and Stewart monarchs from the website of the British monarchy

www.parliament.uk/about/history.cfm
detailed description of the key moments in Parliament's development in Tudor and Stewart times, from the UK Parliament's own website

www.bbc.co.uk/history
illustrated accounts of key moments in the period 1500–1700 with timelines and links to other illustrated sites on themes such as the Reformation, the Gunpowder Plot, the wars of 1637–50 and the Great Fire of 1666

www.scottish.parliament.uk/corporate/history
information about the Treaty of Union of 1707 and the making of the United Kingdom

www.cofe.anglican.org/about/history
description of the development of the Anglican Church, with a focus on the Reformation period

www.thesealedknot.org.uk
timelines and chronology of the civil war in England, with links to related books and articles from the website of the re-enactment society

Index